HILLTOP ELEMENTARY SCHOOL

Good Manners on the Playground

May I ?

by Katie Marsico
illustrated by John Haslam
Content consultant: Robin Gaines Lanzi, PhD, MPH,
Department of Human Science, Georgetown University

magic
wagon

visit us at www.abdopublishing.com

Published by Magic Wagon, a division of the ABDO Group, 8000 West 78th Street, Edina, Minnesota, 55439. Copyright © 2009 by Abdo Consulting Group, Inc. International copyrights reserved in all countries. All rights reserved. No part of this book may be reproduced in any form without written permission from the publisher.

Looking Glass Library™ is a trademark and logo of Magic Wagon.

Printed in the United States of America, North Mankato, Minnesota. 012009 012011

Text by Katie Marsico
Illustrations by John Haslam
Edited by Amy Van Zee
Interior layout and design by Becky Daum
Cover design by Becky Daum

Library of Congress Cataloging-in-Publication Data
Marsico, Katie, 1980-
  Good manners on the playground / by Katie Marsico ; illustrated by John Haslam.
     p. cm. — (Good manners matter!)
  Includes bibliographical references (p.   ).
  ISBN 978-1-60270-612-5
  1. Etiquette for children and teenagers. 2. Playgrounds—Juvenile literature. 3. Play—Juvenile literature. I. Haslam, John. II. Title.
  BJ1857.C5M1269 2009
  395.5'3—dc22

                          2008036316

Contents

Why Do Good Manners Matter on the Playground?

Let's say flying down the slide is your favorite thing to do on the playground. Today there's a long line to use the slide. Should you wait your turn? It would be faster if you pushed the person ahead of you. But you know that wouldn't be the polite thing to do.

You might already know how important it is to have good manners on the playground. If you're polite to people on the playground, everyone can have a good time. Showing others that you care about them is a great way to make friends, too.

It's also good manners to clean up after yourself on the playground. You should place your garbage in a trash can. Also be sure to tell an adult if playground equipment is broken or seems unsafe.

Think about what the playground would be like if no one had good manners. Kids might push and hurt each other. People wouldn't want to take turns. Nobody would care about sharing.

You would never want to go to the playground if people were this rude. How can you show good manners on the playground?

Show Good Manners on the Playground!

Why do you like to visit the playground? Is it because you get to see your friends? Perhaps you enjoy playing outside in the fresh air. Other people go to the playground for the same reason. Always show respect to everyone on the playground. There are many ways to do this.

One important way to show respect is to take turns.
You may want to use the playground equipment.
A lot of kids have the same idea. You can't all swing
on the monkey bars at once or go down the slide
at the same time, though. When you take turns,
everyone gets a chance to play.

If you see a line to play on
a piece of equipment, wait
your turn. Don't cut ahead of
anyone else. This is rude and is
something a bully would do.

Imagine it's your turn to play on the swings. Someone pushes you out of line and takes your turn. How can you use good manners to handle a bully on the playground? Fighting isn't the answer. Try saying, "Excuse me. It was my turn. May I please use the swing?" The person might say she's sorry and step back into line.

If you need help on the playground, look for an adult you know. This could be your mom or dad. It could even be a friend's parent or a teacher. Explain to the adult what's happening. You can also get these people if someone gets hurt.

If someone falls and gets hurt, it's good manners to ask if he or she is okay. Get a grown-up to help if the person is crying or is unable to get up.

You should also show good manners to people besides your friends. Maybe you see the new girl at school sitting alone on a bench. Why not ask her to join your game of tag? It's polite to try to include everyone in the game.

Sharing is another way to practice good manners on the playground. How would you feel if your friends were all eating cookies but didn't offer to share with you?

There are polite words that you can say on the playground. Saying "thank you," "you are welcome," "excuse me," and "please" are ways to practice good manners. You can use these words anywhere to show how polite you are. Let's see some good manners in motion!

Manners in Motion

Lynn and her friend Rob went to the playground after school. They were both waiting in line to use the new seesaw. They were just about to take their turn, but someone cut ahead of them. Lynn saw it was a new boy in their class named Patrick.

"Excuse me," Lynn said to Patrick. "I think we were next in line. May we please use the seesaw?"

Patrick looked embarrassed. "I'm sorry," he answered. "I didn't know there was a line." He turned to walk away.

"No problem, Patrick," said Rob. "Do you want to stay and play with us?" Patrick smiled but seemed unsure.

"How can we?" he asked. "Only two people can ride the seesaw at once."

"We can take turns," Lynn replied. "You and Rob go first. I'll take my turn with one of you afterward."

"Thanks!" said Patrick. "I saved some crackers from my snack at school today. Would either of you like some later?" It was now Lynn and Rob's turn to say thanks.

Can you name all the different ways Lynn, Rob, and Patrick practiced good manners on the playground? It's easy to have good manners! Just remember to be polite and respect the people around you. What good manners have you practiced on the playground lately?

Amazing Facts about Manners on the Playground

Bullies, Beware!

Kids in England know the playground is no place for bullies. In November, England even has a National Anti-Bullying Week! Children of all ages join in events and activities to end bullying. They also try to think of new ways to help people learn respect and good manners.

Playground Parents

Want to do even more to show respect for your local playground? Some schools and towns let people adopt playgrounds. These people help care for the area. They might plant flowers or pick up trash. Talk with your friends and family about adopting a playground near you!

Top Five Tips for Good Manners on the Playground

1. Take turns.
2. Share the equipment.
3. Ask others to join in your games.
4. Don't push or cut in line.
5. Don't forget to say "please," "thank you," and "excuse me!"

Glossary

embarrassed—feeling ashamed or uncomfortable.

equipment—items that are provided for a certain purpose or activity. Playground equipment includes slides and swings.

polite—showing good manners by the way you act or speak.

respect—a sign that you care about people or things and want to treat them well.

rude—showing bad manners by the way you act or speak.

Web Sites

To learn more about manners, visit ABDO Group online at **www.abdopublishing.com**. Web sites about manners are featured on our Book Links page. These links are routinely monitored and updated to provide the most current information available.

Index